Little Mel
Today I'll Change The World

Written By: Robert Damisch

Illustrated By: Lee Edmond Johnson

"Dedicated to the kids with big hearts, who dream big, and want to change the world one day at a time."

- RD

Throwing back the covers and letting out a yawn.

Little Mel jumped out of bed, with pink pajamas on.

Running down the flight of stairs,
she ran up to her mom.

Hugged her quickly, turned around
and switched the TV on.

When she was done she quickly ran upstairs to brush her teeth.

Went to her room, changed her clothes, and started thinking deep.

She reached to pet her puppy, he answered with a twirl.

She then made up her mind and said, "Today I'll change the world."

Her mother overheard her and let out a quiet sigh.

What could this child even do at this tiny age of nine?

She walked up to her daughter, but this she could not say.

Held her close and kissed her head. Then Mel went out to play.

Walking down the sidewalk, a smile upon her face.

"I'm going to change the world," she said, "in each and every place."

As she went on walking, she came across a boy, sitting down, all alone, with a tiny toy.

Little Mel walked up to him and then she blurted out.

"What the heck you crying for, why the need to pout?"

He explained that he was lonely, and wanted to go home.

The problem was that he was scared and could not walk alone.

Laughing out quite loudly, with only this to say,

"Today I'm going to change the world, but I'll help you on the way."

She grabbed his little hand in hers and pulled him to his feet.

With a smile and a bit of laughter, they rushed on down the street.

So when they finally made it, his mom said, "thank the girl."

But Mel had took off running, she had to change the world!

As she kept on walking, she saw a sad old man.

Sitting with some flowers, with tears falling on his hand.

Mel quietly approached him, and asked him what was wrong.

He said that he was stuck here and this was not where he belonged.

He explained quite simply, the place he had to go; his wife was in bed waiting, her time was running low.

He had forgot his wallet and could not take the bus.

Mel reached up, grabbed his hand and said, "Please don't make a fuss."

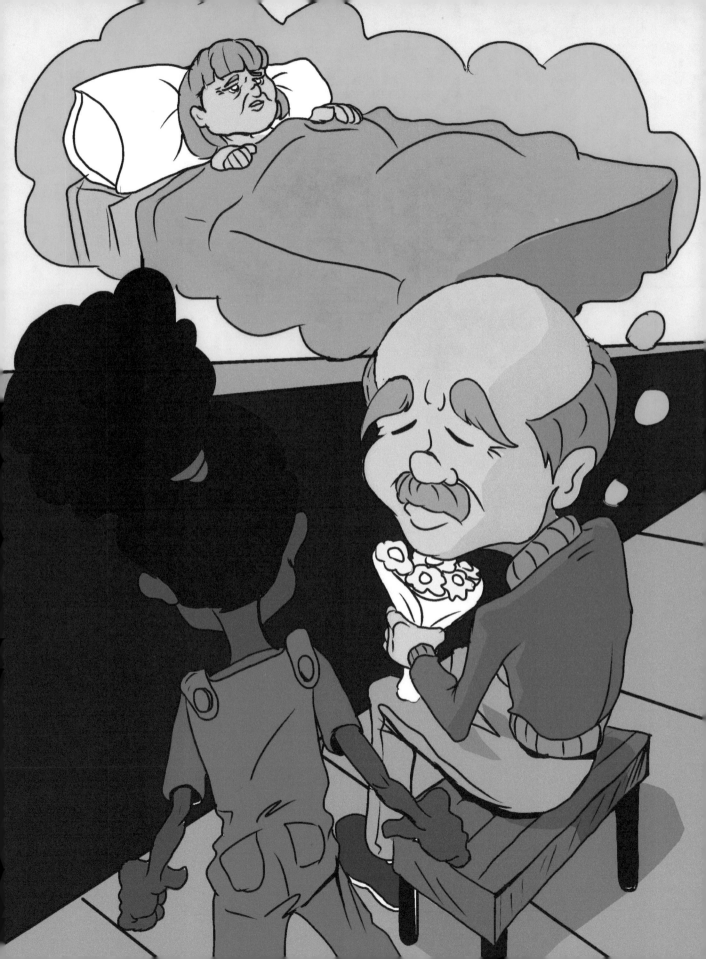

She reached down in her pocket and pulled out fifty cents.

She put it in his hand and said, "I'll cover your expense."

He looked right up to thank her, but she had run away.

"I have to change the world," she said "I only have today."

But she was kept quite busy, with so many things to do.

Every neighbor needed help, she could not just waltz through.

She helped one fix a patio, another seed their lawn.

She carried bags here and there and switched a sprinkler on.

She helped sweep up a drive way, she helped rake up some leaves.

She picked them up, bagged them all, and dirtied up her knees.

The day was almost over and as she began to yawn.

She looked upon the sky and saw the sun was almost gone.

She finally made it home, just as her mom began to worry.

"My little Mel, where have you been? You're oh so sad and dirty."

Mel looked up with tear filled eyes and sadly explained her day.

Her mother listened quietly, not knowing what to say.

"I didn't change the world today," as tears fell from her eyes.

"It has not changed since I woke up" she began sob and cry.

"My darling little angel, my precious little girl

Can't you see what you have done has made a better world?

You helped out where it was needed, gave love out from your heart.

What you did may seem small, but it's the perfect start."

Mel looked up and smiled, and began to understand.

Simple things can change the world, like tiny grains of sand.

So Mel ate up her dinner, cleaned up, and brushed her teeth.

Because of what she did today, she even got a treat.

She got down on her knees and said
a little prayer,

"Thank you God for what you do, and always being there.
I know I'm really tiny, I know I'm only nine.
I know You're really busy and I hope You know that's fine.
Watch over everybody, please take away their fears.
Hold them tight, like each night, and dry away their tears.
God, I want to thank You, for every single friend."

Then like an angel, soft and sweet, she
ended with, "Amen."

Her momma had been listening, and tucked her in her bed.

She wiped her tears and smiled, because of what her daughter said.

She gave her a kiss and finally said,
"My darling little girl.

Sleep now Mel, you've done enough...

You've gone and changed the world..."

THE END

Printed in the USA
CPSIA information can be obtained
at www.ICGtesting.com
LVHW060925181223
766690LV00035B/21